Horses

American Saddlebred Horses

by Kim O'Brien

Consulting Editor: Gail Saunders-Smith, PhD

Capstone
press®

Mankato, Minnesota

Pebble Books are published by Capstone Press,
151 Good Counsel Drive, P.O. Box 669, Mankato, Minnesota 56002.
www.capstonepress.com

Books published by Capstone Press are manufactured with paper
containing at least 10 percent post-consumer waste.

Library of Congress Cataloging-in-Publication Data
O'Brien, Kim, 1960–
    American saddlebred horses / by Kim O'Brien.
    p. cm. — (Pebble books. Horses.)
    Includes bibliographical references and index.
    Summary: "A brief introduction to the characteristics, life cycle, and uses of the
American Saddlebred horse breed" — Provided by publisher.
    ISBN-13: 978-1-4296-3302-4 (library binding)
    1. American saddlebred horse — Juvenile literature. I. Title. II. Series.
SF293.A5O27 2010
636.1'3 — dc22   2008048883

Note to Parents and Teachers

The Horses set supports national science standards related
to life science. This book describes and illustrates the American
Saddlebred horse. The images support early readers in
understanding the text. The repetition of words and phrases helps
early readers learn new words. This book also introduces early
readers to subject-specific vocabulary words, which are defined
in the Glossary section. Early readers may need assistance to read
some words and to use the Table of Contents, Glossary, Read More,
Internet Sites, and Index sections of the book.

Table of Contents

High–Stepping Horse 5

Show Horses 9

From Foal to Adult 13

A Favorite Horse 17

Glossary 22

Read More 23

Internet Sites 23

Index 24

4

High-Stepping Horse

American Saddlebreds
are graceful horses.
They hold their heads
high when they move.

Saddlebreds have
large, kind eyes.
They have pointed ears.

Show Horses

Saddlebreds are show horses. They do a prancing movement called a slow gait.

Saddlebreds also learn
a fast movement
called a rack.

From Foal to Adult

Saddlebred foals stay close to their mothers.

They weigh about 100 pounds (45 kilograms) when they are born.

Adult Saddlebreds
stand 15 to 17 hands tall.
They weigh about
1000 pounds
(454 kilograms).

Horses are measured in hands.
Each hand is 4 inches (10 centimeters).
A horse is measured from the ground
to its withers.

A Favorite Horse

Saddlebreds are good dressage horses. Dressage horses move in a controlled way.

Saddlebreds are
harness horses.
They pull carts in shows.

Saddlebreds are friendly and hardworking horses. People enjoy riding them.

Glossary

breed — a group of animals that come from common relatives

cart — a small wagon with two wheels

dressage — the art of guiding a horse through different movements

foal — a young horse

gait — a way of moving

harness — a set of leather straps that connect a horse to a cart or wagon

prance — to walk or move in a lively or proud way

show horse — a horse that competes in a contest for a prize

Read More

Fetty, Margaret. *Show Horses.* Horse Power. New York: Bearport, 2007.

Harper, Dan. *Horses A-Z.* An A to Z Encyclopedia. San Diego, Calif.: Blackbirch Press, 2006.

Internet Sites

FactHound offers a safe, fun way to find Internet sites related to this book. All of the sites on FactHound have been researched by our staff.

Here's what you do:

Visit *www.facthound.com*

FactHound will fetch the best sites for you!

Index

adults, 15

carts, 19

dressage, 17

ears, 7

eyes, 7

foals, 13

hands, 15

harness, 19

heads, 5

movements, 5, 9, 11, 17

prancing, 9

rack, 11

shows, 9, 19

slow gait, 9

weight, 13, 15

withers, 15

Word Count: 108
Grade: 1
Early-Intervention Level: 18

Editorial Credits
Sarah L. Schuette, editor; Bobbi J. Wyss, designer; Jo Miller, media researcher

Photo Credits
Alamy/tbkmedia.de, 8
Capstone Press/TJ Thoraldson Digital Photography, cover, 1, 4, 6, 10, 12, 14, 16, 20
Yvonne Scott Photography/Seth Scott, 18

The author dedicates this book in memory of her grandmother, Katherine Boulware Sutton.